CITIES

CITIES

through the eyes of artists

The Metropolitan Museum of Art, New York

Wendy and Jack Richardson

MACMILLAN

First published 1989

Published by Macmillan Children's Books
A division of MACMILLAN PUBLISHERS LTD.
Houndmills, Basingstoke, Hampshire RG21 2XS and London

Companies and representatives throughout the world

Picture research by Faith Perkins

Printed in Italy

British Library Cataloguing in Publication Data

Richardson, Wendy
Cities.
1. Graphic arts. Special subjects
Urban regions. Social life
I. Title II. Richardson, Jack III. Series
760'. 044909091732

ISBN 0-333-47570-4

Photographic acknowledgements

The authors and publishers wish to acknowledge with thanks the following photographic sources:

Cover: Sydney Harbour – Ken Done © 1986
Beer Street – The Mary Evans Picture Library piii
Georgia O'Keeffe – The Metropolitan Museum of Art, New York pvi
Canaletto – Anglesey Abbey (Fotomas Index) p8
The Basin of St Marco – The National Gallery, London p9
Patrick Procktor – Photograph by Duncan Baxter p10
Bacino – © Patrick Procktor, The Redfern Gallery, London p11
El Greco – The Metropolitan Museum of Art, Purchase, Joseph Pulitzer Bequest, 1924 p12
View of Toledo – The Metropolitan Museum of Art, request of Mrs H. O. Havemeyer, 1929. The H. O. Havemeyer Collection p13
Daumier – The Phillips Collection, Washington DC (Visual Arts Library) p14
Third-Class Carriage – The Metropolitan Museum of Art, request of Mrs H. O. Havemeyer, 1929. The H. O. Havemeyer Collection p15
Monet – The Tate Gallery, London © DACS 1988 p16
La Gare St Lazare – Musée D'Orsay, Paris © DACS 1988 (Lauros-Giraudon/Bridgeman Art Library) p17
Severini – Private Collection © DACS 1988 (Visual Arts Library) p18
Suburban Trains Arriving in Paris – The Tate Gallery, London © ADAGP, Paris and DACS, London 1988 p19
Ford Maddox Brown – National Portrait Gallery, London p20
Work – City of Manchester Art Gallery p21
Graham Sutherland – The National Portrait Gallery, London p22
Teeming Pit – Imperial War Museum, London p23
Lowry – Salford Art Gallery and Museum. Reproduced by courtesy of Mrs Carol Ann Danes (The Bridgeman Art Library) p24
Ancoats Hospital – The Whitworth Art Gallery, University of Manchester. Reproduced by courtesy of Mrs Carol Ann Danes p25
Renoir – Musée D'Orsay, Paris (Lauros-Giraudon/Bridgeman Art Library) p26
Le Moulin de la Galette – John Hay Whitney Collection, New York (The Bridgeman Art Library) p27
George Bellows – National Academy of Design, New York p28
Cliff Dwellers – Los Angeles County Museum of Art. Museum Purchase with Los Angeles County Funds p29
Men in the City – Peggy Guggenheim Collection Venice , The Solomon R. Guggenheim Foundation © DACS 1988 p31
Charles Sheeler – National Portrait Gallery, Smithsonian Institution Washington DC p32
Skyscrapers – The Phillips Collection, Washington DC p33
Georgia O'Keeffe – The Metropolitan Museum of Art, New York p34
The East River from Shelton – New Jersey State Museum Collection. Purchased by the Association for the Arts of New Jersey State Museum with a gift from Mary Lea Johnson p35
Frank Auerbach – Photograph, Marlborough Fine Art, London p36
Looking Toward Mornington Crescent – Graves Art Gallery, Sheffield. Marlborough Fine Art, London p37
L'Ambrosiano – Recordi Collection, Milan p39
Urban Ointment – © DACS 1988 (The Bridgeman Art Library) p41
Bridal Accessories – The Allan Stone Gallery, New York (The Bridgeman Art Library) p43
Ken Done – Photograph Mark Lang/Wildlight Photo Agency p44
Sydney Harbour – Ken Done © 1986 p45
Making of a Fresco – The San Francisco Art Institute, California p47

The publishers have made every effort to trace the copyright holders, but if they have inadvertently overlooked any, they will be pleased to make the necessary arrangement at the first opportunity.

Introduction

This is a book of pictures about cities. Some of the pictures are old and some of them were made quite recently. They come from all over the world. Some are paintings, some are drawings, some are prints. Some come from books, some are on walls and some are made to hang on walls. They look very different, but they have one thing in common. They were made by people who had an idea about life in the city and thought that the best way to share that idea was through a picture. So this is a book for you to look at.

The pictures tell how the artists felt about the cities that people have built. They look at city streets, at homes and shops and factories, and they also look at people at work and at play in these cities.

You will see how differently the city environment has made each of the artists feel, and you will have different feelings as you look at each of the pictures. Some of the pictures you may agree with because you feel the same way. Others may show the city world as something quite different from the way you see it.

You may not be a city dweller. If you live in a village or a small town you will probably see the city from quite a different point of view. Take a careful look at the pictures and see if you feel the same way as the painters about city life.

Contents

The Basin of St Marco on Ascension Day

Oil on canvas 121.9 × 182.8cm

Giovanni Antonio Canal (known as Canaletto)

Anglesey Abbey

LIVED:
c.1697-1768

NATIONALITY:
Italian

TYPE OF WORK:
oil paintings

Antonio Canal worked with his father and brother in Venice, designing and painting scenery for the theatre. In 1719 he accompanied his father to Rome to paint sets for the composer Scarlatti. Whilst there he decided to concentrate on painting pictures. He stayed in Rome for about two years, but was back in Venice by 1720 when his name appeared in a list of the Professional Guild of Painters of Venice. By 1732 Antonio Canal, now known as Canaletto, was rich and famous.

The city of water

Venice is a most unusual city, built on several islands in a lagoon. Its main streets are canals, and smaller canals thread between the houses and courtyards. There are no hills in Venice, so the skies seem huge and the horizon is far away. With so much water around, there are always rippling reflections. Canaletto explored every corner of Venice. He painted the great squares and palaces and the quiet corners and narrow backwaters.

Painting the real world

Canaletto's work changed the tradition of 'view painting'. He painted the magnificent architecture in accurate detail but he managed to fill his pictures with more than cold facts. He painted the city so that we can feel the warmth of the Mediterranean sunshine and enjoy its light dappling the water under the great dome of the sky. In the clear light the city takes on a serene beauty which may be a rather romantic view of life at that time.

This large painting of the Grand Canal and the Doge's Palace, shows us the beginning of an important ceremony called The Wedding of the Sea. The ruler of Venice, the Doge, is about to board a special barge. He will be rowed out into the lagoon where he will throw a ring into the water to bless Venice's navy and the cargo boats on which the city's trade depends.

The National Gallery, London

Bacino

Aquatint, four colours 65.7 × 89.4 cm

Patrick Procktor

Photograph by Duncan Baxter

BORN:
1936

NATIONALITY:
born in Ireland. Came to England aged four.

TYPE OF WORK:
prints, watercolours, oil paintings

Patrick Procktor and Canaletto must have been standing on almost the same spot when they made their pictures of the Doge's Palace across the water.

At first glance the pictures are very different. This is partly because they are made quite differently. Canaletto painted his picture with a brush. Procktor's picture is drawn on copper plates. It is an aquatint. Both pictures show the same huge sky, though, and the rippling water and the brilliance of everything that the sunlight touches.

Procktor went to Venice with the printer Charles Newington. The painter produced forty watercolours which were exhibited in a gallery in Venice and sold instantly. Charles Newington had taken photographs of the paintings, and it was from these that they worked together to produce a series of seven prints.

The technique

The drawings were made on two copper plates which were covered in resin. The lines of the drawings were cut into the plates using acid. Then ink was brushed over the plates and the pictures were printed on to paper. This process was repeated four times using different coloured inks. Each print is placed exactly on top of the next. Can you see where each colour has been printed? For this picture Procktor used grey, blue, brown and red.

View of Toledo

Oil on canvas 121 × 109 cm

Domenicos Theotocopoulos
(known as 'El Greco', the Greek)

LIVED:
c.1544-1614

NATIONALITY:
Greek, but worked in Italy and Spain

TYPE OF WORK:
oil paintings

The Metropolitan Museum of Art, Purchase,
Joseph Pulitzer Request, 1924

El Greco was born on the Greek island of Crete. He studied in Venice with the painters Tintoretto and Titian. He moved to Spain where he was given his Spanish name. El Greco spent the rest of his working life in Toledo, in southern Spain.

Painting feelings

This painting would not help anyone trying to find their way in Toledo! El Greco was a painter more concerned with atmosphere and emotion than with visual accuracy. In this painting he has changed things to suit his own design. He has painted the cathedral on the wrong side of the castle. He shows some buildings from the front and others from the side.

The city sits on top of the hill. The spire of the cathedral and the bulk of the castle rise into the sky. What a sky it is! A fearful storm is about to burst. Yet the tiny people (you will have to look very hard to see them) do not seem to be worried by the weather. They are busy in the fields or down by the river. They do not seem to be hurrying as they walk up the hill to the gatehouse. It is almost as if they do not see the threatening skies.

El Greco did not paint the portrait of a city as Canaletto did. He was trying to say something about what was going on in the city. The cathedral and the castle are symbols of the power of the church and of the state. Is the painting trying to tell of their stormy partnership? The people, as ordinary people do everywhere, are just getting on with their lives. They have no power to change the battle going on above them any more than they can change the weather.

A painter's tricks

El Greco uses all sorts of painter's tricks to make us look up. The river and roads curl upwards. He altered the gatehouse towers so that the taller one is at the back and our eyes go on up the line of architecture. We are looking at the city not so much from far away as from well below it. We look up to the conflict on the hill.

The Third-Class Carriage

Oil on canvas 65.5 × 90 cm

Honoré Daumier

LIVED:
c.1808-1879

NATIONALITY:
French

TYPE OF WORK:
lithographs, engravings, watercolours, oil paintings

The Phillips Collection, Washington DC

When Honoré Daumier died in 1897 he left more pictures than any other known artist. He made about three thousand lithographs for newspapers, about one thousand wood engravings, eight hundred watercolours and three hundred oil paintings. Daumier earned his living until he was fifty-two years old drawing illustrations and cartoons for the newspapers in Paris. At that time photographs could not be easily reproduced. All the time though he wanted to spend more time painting. His chance came when he lost his job.

The cartoonist turns to painting

For three years Daumier struggled to make a living from painting. He had studied the sculptures in the Louvre Museum in Paris, but he had no formal training in the techniques of oil painting. He tried to work on canvas in the way that he had on stone for his lithographs, smudging paint into areas of light and darkness and making his shapes by drawing. We can see the influence of his sculpture studies. The heads of his figures have a stonelike quality but they are also very much alive.

Comments on the times

Daumier's newspaper work was very often sharp comment on the politics and politicians of the day. His paintings also are comments on the life he saw around him. Here we see the working people of Paris in a crowded railway carriage. In 1864, a few years before this was painted, he had published a cartoon showing a similar railway carriage scene. Under it was the caption 'Hurrah for third-class carriages where one might die from lack of air but never from assassination'.

What do you think he meant by this caption? Did he paint this picture with the same feelings?

The Metropolitan Museum of Art, request of Mrs H. O. Havemeyer, 1929. The H. O. Havemeyer Collection

La Gare St Lazare

Oil on canvas 75 × 100 cm
Claude Monet

LIVED:
1840-1926

NATIONALITY:
French

TYPE OF WORK:
oil paintings, drawings

The Tate Gallery, London © DACS 1988

Claude Monet is probably the painter most people think of first when the Impressionists are mentioned. They were a group of French artists who lived in and around Paris and worked quite closely together for several years, sharing their ideas and often travelling together to paint.

A new vision

Monet said that he would like to paint as a bird sings, and also that he would like to have been born blind, then to gain his sight just as he was ready to start painting, so that he saw things for the first time without knowing what they were. From the style of painting that he chose and developed throughout his long career, we can begin to see what Monet meant. He wanted to see everything around him naturally and with fresh eyes. He tried to get away from the old ideas about how to paint the world.

More than one glance

Sometimes Monet painted a series of pictures about one subject. This picture *La Gare St Lazare* [St Lazare Station] is one of eight canvases which he showed in the Impressionists' exhibition in 1877. Each of the paintings shows the sheds and tracks outside the station from different angles.

Careful consideration

Monet may have wanted to paint naturally but that did not mean that he did not think carefully about every aspect of his work. For instance he chose very carefully the colours with which he prepared, or primed, his canvas, sometimes choosing white, sometimes warm creamy shades or pale greys. The colour was always light so that the paint he applied to it had a luminous glow.

Parts of a whole

Monet tried in these paintings to see and paint the scene as one whole object. The parts within it, the human figures, the engine, the sheds, the puffs of smoke, are there, but they merge together. His thick brush marks create a pattern of colour in which we read a picture. He was able to weave a rich texture of gleaming light and shadowy darkness.

Musée D'Orsay, Paris © DACS 1988

Suburban Trains Arriving in Paris

Oil on canvas 87 × 116 cm

Gino Severini

Private Collection © DACS 1988

LIVED:
1883-1966

NATIONALITY:
Italian

TYPE OF WORK:
oil paintings

The childhood and youth of Gino Severini was a long hard struggle for survival. He came from a very poor family and lived for a time with his grandfather. At about seventeen Severini was living alone in Rome, struggling to learn to paint. In 1906 he sold some copies of religious paintings to a tourist in Florence and used the money to travel to Paris. There he met fellow Italian Modigliani who introduced him to Picasso and his friends. At that time, this group of artists were painting in a style called Cubism. Severini was also impressed with the work of the Impressionist painter Seurat, and he experimented with his style, putting tiny dots of paint onto the canvas.

In 1910, while Severini was working in Paris, a group of young Italian painters wrote down their ideas about art in a modern technological world. Their ideas, known as Futurism, were based on the writings of a poet called Marinetti. They urged young painters to try out anything new, and to stop looking at the past. They thought that copying old ideas was a waste of time. The young men came to Paris and Severini introduced them to the Cubists. Severini began to work in a way which merged Futurist ideas with the style of the Cubists and the techniques of Seurat.

Speed and aggression

Severini painted this in 1915. The houses and factories that the train has come racing past are shown as very simple shapes with little detail. They are arranged higgledy-piggledy, which is the impression you get from the window of a speeding train. Smoke billows and envelops the city. The train seems to be both moving and at a standstill at its city destination.

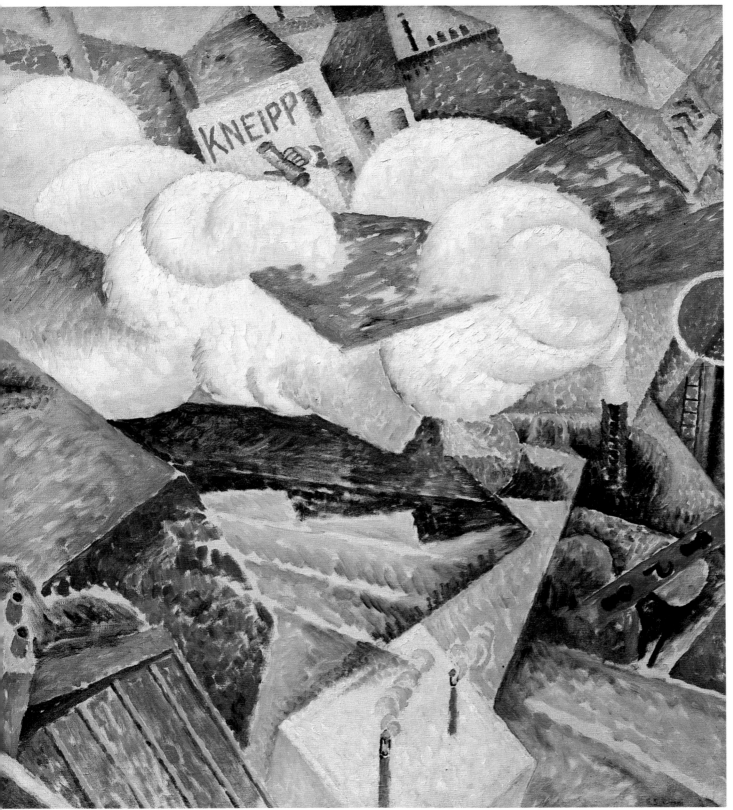

Work

Oil on canvas 137 × 197.3cm
Ford Madox Brown

National Portrait Gallery, London

LIVED:
1821-1893

NATIONALITY:
English. Born in Calais, grew up in Belgium, moved to England

TYPE OF WORK:
oil paintings, furniture, stained glass

Ford Madox Brown grew up and was trained as a painter in Belgium. In 1844 he came to live in London, where a few years later he met Dante Gabriel Rosetti and a group of artists known as the Pre-Raphaelite Brotherhood.

The style of the Brotherhood

Madox Brown agreed with the group's ideas about art but never actually joined them. He tried out some of their techniques and like them he worked out of doors in natural light, painting in clear bright colours.

A real incident as a start to the picture

Madox Brown saw a group of men digging the road and drew them. The idea for the painting grew from the drawing. It is called *Work* and it reflects some of the social problems of the time. In the centre of the picture are the navvies digging up the road. They represent physical work. On the left of them, in rags, is a poor creature who has no chance of work. Behind him are two rich ladies. One of them is trying to help the poor by offering good advice. She holds a booklet on the evils of drink called 'The Hodmans Haven, or drink for thirsty souls'. Just behind them is another worker carrying a tray of cakes. He is a symbol of their riches. They can eat bread and cakes. At the top of the picture are the upper classes, a father and daughter on horseback. At the bottom of the picture the poorest class, a ragged orphan family, are kept in order by a skinny child of ten. Huddled under the trees are Irish immigrants seeking work. On the other side of the street the police move on a poor orange-seller. On the right of the picture are two men who seem to be idle. They represent 'brain work' and are two well known 'thinkers' of the day. Everyone in the picture is a real person. Madox Brown hired Irish labourers to pose for him and the dirty baby is his own child.

SEEST THOU A MAN DILIGENT IN
HIS BUSINESS? HE SHALL
STAND BEFORE KINGS.

City of Manchester Art Gallery

Teeming Pit

Ink, gouache and chalk on paper 49.5 × 37cm

Graham Sutherland

LIVED:
1903-1980

NATIONALITY:
British

TYPE OF WORK:
portraits, etchings, tapestries, drawings, posters

The National Portrait Gallery, London

Graham Sutherland became an engineering apprentice at the Midland Railway Works before changing his mind about a career and enrolling at Goldsmiths College in London to study art. He specialised first in engraving and did not begin to paint seriously until he was twenty-seven years old. Many of his early paintings are of country scenes. It was in the country that he learned to look. In a conversation with a writer friend in 1963 he said: 'As a child . . . I went out into the country a great deal. I was often alone. I got into the habit of looking at things very closely – observing, analysing and drawing everything in the countryside'.

Drawing on past experience

During the Second World War, Sutherland became an official war artist. He was asked to record life in Britain, first in London in the Blitz and then in the industrial valleys of South Wales. Sutherland was able to draw on his own experience as an apprentice to help him to understand the lives of some of the people he painted.

'I have always liked and been fascinated by the primitiveness of heavy engineering shops and their vast floors. In a way they are cathedrals.'

Perhaps we can see what he meant in this drawing called *Teeming Pit: Tapping a Steel Furnace.* The furnace is a huge cauldron in a vast building. We cannot see its walls. The fires which heat the iron ore to melting point billow from the cauldron mouth creating dramatic contrasts of light and darkness. The men at work are seen in the glow from the molten metal. They are not individuals with faces but they are not robots either. They are the workforce. They are drawn as simple, strong shapes. There is something dance-like in their movement as they reach and bend. Sutherland spoke of 'the rite they performed' like priests or performers at a ceremony going through well rehearsed actions. They celebrate the mystery of the liquid steel pouring from the furnace.

Sutherland does not see industry in a mechanical way. He seems to see the manufactured shapes as growing, living objects.

Sutherland 1942.

Imperial War Museum, London

Ancoats Hospital Outpatients Department

Oil on canvas 59.3 × 90 cm

L. S. Lowry

LIVED:
1887-1976

NATIONALITY:
British

TYPE OF WORK:
oil paintings, drawings

Salford Art Gallery and Museum. Reproduced by courtesy of Mrs Carol Ann Danes

Lawrence Stephen Lowry was born in Manchester and attended art school there and in Salford when the family moved. The industrial scene was the landscape he knew and its workers were the people he grew up with.

A simple man

Lowry said of himself: 'I am a simple man and I use simple materials: ivory black, vermillion, Prussian blue, yellow ochre, flake white and no medium. That's all I've ever used for my painting. I like oils. Watercolours I've used only occasionally. They don't really suit me: dry too quickly.'

Lowry's 'simple' painting was done with a variety of tools. He put the paint on thickly with a brush or a palette knife. Then sometimes he would rub it away, or scratch through the surface with a nail. He usually painted on a white background, but the white would be changed to be gentle and creamy or sharp and bright.

Lowry's people

This painting was commissioned for Ancoats Hospital. It is a typical Lowry painting, full of the people he knew so well. They are sometimes called 'matchstick' people, but they are very much more than that. Look at the two women in the centre front. They are enjoying a gossip while they wait. The men on either side of them wait patiently but are bored. It is because of his knowledge of the way people sit and stand and lean and rest that Lowry's people are so real. Small groups dot the picture. They make us curious to know what is going on. What is wrong with the very pale man lying on the stretcher? We can almost hear the conversations and feel as if we are there waiting for the doctor to call us in. Lowry has achieved this through his design. The benches and the people in lines lead us down the long room. There is even a space for us to walk past them to get to the office at the back.

The Whitworth Art Gallery, University of Manchester. Reproduced by courtesy of Mrs Carol Ann Danes

Ball at the Moulin de la Galette

Oil on canvas 120 × 94 cm
Pierre Auguste Renoir

Musée D'Orsay, Paris.

LIVED:
1841-1919

NATIONALITY:
French

TYPE OF WORK:
portraits, landscapes, still life

Pierre Auguste Renoir was the sixth child in a family of seven. His parents were a tailor and a dress-maker, and young Pierre was apprenticed to learn a trade too. He learnt to paint on porcelain, but before he was qualified, the demand for his craft dropped.

Turning to painting

In 1862 Renoir began to study painting at art college. He had very definite ideas about paintings. He once told a friend: 'Painting is done to decorate walls, so it should be as rich as possible. For me a picture should be something likeable, joyous and pretty – yes pretty. There are enough ugly things in life for us not to add to them. I like painting which I can stroll in to stroke the cat.'

An afternoon in Paris

Renoir lived not far from this open-air dance hall in an area of Paris called Montmartre and he painted this scene on the spot. We see the dance hall in the dappled light of a sunny afternoon. The group in the foreground sit in the shade of a tree and the light, filtered through leaves, flickers on coats and dresses and makes the whole painting shimmer. Renoir, like Monet, was interested in the effect produced by painting small dabs of colour which give an impression of a picture. The Impressionists often chose everyday scenes to paint, and were particularly interested in how natural light changed the scene at different times of day.

Look at the little people in the background. Renoir has used the trick of diminishing scale to set the back of the picture far from the front, but he also creates the effect by painting the far away figures as fleeting impressions. We cannot see clearly what is so far off.

We are seeing only a part of the scene at the dance hall. It is not a posed scene in a studio but the real thing. On both sides of the painting are incomplete figures. The man in the foreground has his back to us. We are passers-by catching a glimpse of a happy afternoon in the city. There may not be a cat to stroke, but we can definitely stroll in this picture.

John Hay Whitney Collection, New York.

Cliff Dwellers

Oil on canvas 100 × 105 cm
George Wesley Bellows

LIVED:
1882-1925

NATIONALITY:
American

TYPE OF WORK:
oil paintings

National Academy of Design, New York

In the nineteenth century, North American artists looked to Europe as the centre of the art world. Many of them came to the academies of Europe to train. With the new century came a new pride and determination to be American. Painters began to look at, and to paint, places and ideas that were part of the cultural development of the United States.

The Ashcan Group

George Wesley Bellows was a larger-than-life character, full of vitality. He was part of a group who were known as the Ashcan painters. At first the critics and public disliked their work. They were used to paintings of beautiful things, flowers and landscapes, or aristocratic portraits. They did not care for these paintings of ordinary people in their real surroundings, so they exaggerated a little and talked of the group who painted ashcans or rubbish bins.

A clever comparison

In *Cliff Dwellers*, Bellows compares the city buildings reaching up into the sky with cliffs on the sea shore, and the inhabitants of the buildings with the sea birds who make their nests on the cliff ledges. It is a clever comparison. The balconies are busy with the activity of the city dwellers who try to get a little air in the hot summer. It is a noisy scene. We can imagine neighbours calling to one another from apartment to apartment. The scene at street level is rather like a beach below the cliffs. Adults sit in the evening sun on doorsteps and pavements. The children play or rest in the shade. But in the middle of this 'beach' a street car goes by on the road crowded with traffic.

This is not a scene that could be called beautiful in the way of the traditional landscape painters, but it is full of life and vitality. It seems obvious that Bellows liked city people and wanted to celebrate their energy.

Men in the City

Oil on canvas 145.7 × 113.5 cm

Fernand Léger

LIVED:
1881-1955

NATIONALITY:
French

TYPE OF WORK:
oil paintings, film and stage design, murals, ceramics

Fernand Léger was a painter who was excited by the new life in the cities of the twentieth century. For two or three years he made paintings which were about new technology and mechanisation. Everything in his pictures he turned into geometric shapes and machine-like parts.

Putting the parts together

At first the picture may seem confusing. If you look at parts of it, one at a time, it is hard to make sense of the whole thing. Yet if you take it all in in one look it is very clearly of three men in the city. Perhaps the confusion was part of Léger's plan. Cities are confusing places until you get to know them.

The men look as if they are made from tubing. They are more like robots than real people. Their faces are nearly featureless. It would be very hard to recognise them if you met them anywhere else. They have lost their individuality and identity.

The city the men are in is made up of blocks that are organised in a very orderly pattern. No part looks like any real thing, and yet it is possible to see roofs and balconies, windows and doorways, and even inside the buildings, boilers and machinery. Yet none of it is really there. It is all just suggested by the use of colour and shape. It is not a threatening new world, though. The colours are bold and exciting and warm us rather than coldly frightening us. Their clear-edged shapes are placed so that they have a bold impact. Black, white and red dominate. The paler colours seem to make the picture more solid. They also remind us of more traditional building materials.

A new way of thinking about art

Léger, like many painters at the beginning of the century, was trying to find new ways to express new ideas. Some of these artists were involved in the Cubist movement. They were interested in colour and shape for its own sake, and thought that a picture could be interesting and perhaps beautiful just because of the way the parts in it were arranged. Some of Léger's paintings are more abstract than this one, which has distorted objects to express an idea but is still quite easily readable.

Skyscrapers

Oil on canvas 63.5 × 82 cm

Charles Sheeler

LIVED:
1883-1965

NATIONALITY:
American

TYPE OF WORK:
oil paintings, drawings,
photography

National Portrait Gallery, Smithsonian Institution, Washington DC

Charles Sheeler was born in Pennsylvania and studied at the Philadelphia School of Industrial Art and then at the Pennsylvania Academy and in Europe. He experimented with many of the new ideas about painting that were being discussed and tried out in Europe. Then with other North American painters he developed a style that came to be called Precisionism or Mechanism. The style started with work similar to the style of the Cubist painters. Léger's paintings may have influenced these painters. However, the bold new architecture of New York and the atmosphere of industrial and commercial growth and orderliness played their part in the development of the American style. So did an interest in experimental photography. Many painters including Sheeler used photography to express their ideas and to help them develop their paintings.

The cold precision of the new city

This painting is typical of the Precisionist style. It is coldly exact, or precise, and has a strong solidity. The towering blocks with their clean efficiency are real enough and yet the city has an unlived-in look. The great height of New York buildings is felt as well as shown. We are looking down from one building onto the roofs of others. We cannot see the street. The life of the city is going on way down below us. We look up to other roof tops.

We cannot see how this picture has been painted. There is no thickness to the paint, nor any of the marks of the brush. The areas of colour are flat and sunlit or shaded walls are set at angles to each other to give us the solidity of the buildings. Dark shadows make the painting more solid too, and remind us that the city is part of nature after all.

The Phillips Collection, Washington DC

East River from Shelton

Oil on canvas 63.7 × 55.8 cm

Georgia O'Keeffe

LIVED:
1887-1986

NATIONALITY:
American

TYPE OF WORK:
oil paintings, drawings,

Metropolitan Museum of Art, New York

Georgia O'Keeffe made up her mind to be an artist when she was ten years old. When she grew up, she went to art college in Chicago and worked as a commercial artist and as a teacher of art. She continued to study painting until one day in 1915, when she was twenty-eight years old, she gathered her work together in one room and looked at it all carefully. She decided that she had learned nothing of value, so she destroyed everything and started again. She was determined to peel off all the layers of learning that had prevented her from doing what she really wanted to, and to find her own way of painting.

Finding her style

In New York she met other painters and became part of the Precisionist group. But her paintings were always different and showed a very personal style.

Though this painting has something in common with *Skyscrapers* (page 33) its view of the city is not as cold and hard. O'Keeffe's work is in some ways decorative and romantic. The city is more than its buildings for her. The factories across the river belch out smoke that forms a swirling cloud, masking the sun and making a distinct pattern. The buildings on this side are harshly silhouetted against the water and add their smoke to the mass above.

This painting shows how the Precisionists were influenced by photography. At first glance it could be a photograph. We cannot see much evidence of paint. But yet the picture has an unreal feeling. There is something magical about the painting despite its down-to-earth subject.

Looking towards Mornington Crescent station – Night

Oil on board 122 × 122 cm

Frank Auerbach

BORN:
1931

NATIONALITY:
Born in Germany. Came to England as a child.

TYPE OF WORK:
oil paintings

Photograph Marlborough Fine Art, London

Frank Auerbach was born in Berlin but before his eighth birthday he was sent to England when Germany became a Fascist state. He never saw his family or anyone he had known in Germany again. When he was seventeen years old he came to London thinking he might become an actor, but he went to St Martin's School of Art instead and then to the Royal Academy. He has worked in the same London studio since leaving the Academy.

Beginning again

Auerbach's paintings take many months and sometimes years to complete because he keeps starting them again. He does not just make changes, but scrapes the paint right off and begins again. He works very quickly and for long hours at a time. The new work might be very different from the one it replaces, but it is still the same painting. Auerbach says that each time he paints he learns something new about the subject and it needs to be painted differently. He says that he looks at each painting after a night's rest and knows either that it is finished or that he must begin again.

Paint in liquid layers

You can see the thickness of the paint in this picture of a London street at night. It is a large painting, about 1.22 metres square. You can see that the paint has been put on with wide sweeps of a large brush. No wonder Auerbach says that he finds painting very tiring! Despite the heaviness of the paint and the obvious brush marks, the whole picture glows in the artificial light. The buildings are great masses of paint, darkly green or blue, or luminously orange. Their doors and windows are black holes. The painting has an exciting air about it.

How does the way Auerbach uses paint make you feel? Do you feel excited by the picture? Does the city he paints seem like a real place to you?

L'Ambrosiano

Screen print

Mario Sironi

LIVED:
1885-1961

NATIONALITY:
Italian

TYPE OF WORK:
oil paintings, murals

Like Gino Severini, Mario Sironi was a member of the
Futurist movement in Italy. He had started training as
an engineer before turning to painting and meeting the
Futurists. Sironi wanted art to be a part of the modern
world and he celebrated all that was modern in his
pictures. Sironi's subjects were usually city and factory
made objects, such as trucks and bicycles.

Creating an impact

Sironi uses bold flat areas of colour to create impact in this
poster advertising the evening edition of a city newspaper.
An energetic newsboy steps towards us with the latest
news hot off the presses in his arms. Perhaps we can grab a
paper from his hand as he rushes past. He is in a hurry while
the news is fresh.

The brilliant red has the same effect on us as a fire engine
racing towards us would have. It makes a great visual
noise! The muted greens behind it enhance the brilliance of
the red. Yellow, the colour known to attract our attention
most, is used to make sure we know which newspaper he is
carrying. He seems to be emerging from the very heart of
the city where everything is happening. He must know
what is going on. Behind him skyscraper buildings
emphasise the up-to-dateness of the newspaper.

An influence from the past

The poster uses a style invented by the French painter
Toulouse-Lautrec. His influence on advertising is still to be
seen today and his posters are as popular now as they were
when new a hundred years ago.

EDIZIONE
DEL
POMERIGGIO

L'Ambrosiano

Urban Ointment

Solvent transfer on fabric collaged to paper

Robert (Milton) Rauschenberg

BORN:
1925

NATIONALITY:
American

TYPE OF WORK:
paintings, collages, assemblages, sculptures, theatre sets, costumes

Robert Rauschenberg is an artist who is interested in city life, and in the objects and ideas that are used and abandoned in cities as they move in and out of fashion.

Rauschenberg grew up in Texas and began studies in pharmacy but was expelled from the university. While in the navy he saw original paintings for the first time at a museum in California and when his military service was over he studied art in Kansas, Carolina and Paris. He moved to New York in 1949 and began to experiment with new ways of making pictures. He added to painting a number of unusual techniques such as photographic silk-screen printing combined with drawing, transfer and collage. He makes sculptures as well. One of his most famous is of a stuffed goat wearing a car tyre.

Found materials

Rauschenberg uses images and objects of all sorts in his work. He has said: 'A pair of socks is no less suitable to make a painting than wood, nails, turpentine, oil and fabric.'

This painting is called *Urban Ointment*. It combines an odd assortment of photographs; a boat in icy waters, a skeleton on a stand, American footballers, city street scenes, a hair care advertisement and a baby eagle. These pictures are cut and rearranged and joined by long printed strips which run over or through them. They are linked together by colour, too. The pale yellow on which they are placed is echoed in several of the pictures within the picture.

The picture is intriguing to look at. It is also interesting to try to read it like a book. What might be the meaning, if there is one, hidden in all these pictures? What made Rauschenberg choose to combine this particular set of photographs and drawings?

Technology

Rauschenberg is very interested in new technology. His pictures are made using modern techniques. In 1969 he said: 'By working together sharing information, technology and art could be a way of awakening the conscience of people to avoid a crucial disaster.'

Do you think this picture, which was made in 1980, was intended to have a message like that?

Bridal Accessories

Oil on canvas 91.5 × 122 cm
Richard Estes

BORN:
1936

NATIONALITY:
American

TYPE OF WORK:
oil paintings

Richard Estes makes his paintings from colour photographs. He usually works from transparencies. He and other painters who work in the same way are known as the Super Realists. They make paintings which are more like photographs than photographs!

Estes' work shows street scenes in New York City. It is frequently of office blocks and buildings or of shop windows. He likes angles and reflections. He rarely paints people even though it is the city life which interests him.

What do you think Estes found special about this street scene? It is quiet and empty. The shops are closed and barred. Only an empty drinks can and oddments of litter in the gutter tell us that people have been around. Perhaps it was the strangeness of the shop window with its rows of heads and hats that caught his attention. Perhaps it was the light catching the glass and the aluminium and the reflected buildings from the other side of the street.

Look carefully at a photograph of shops in a city (perhaps you can find one in a magazine), or take a long look at the shops in your local high street and compare it with Estes' painting. Does the painting look real to you or has everything been neatened up? Does the Super Real painting tell you anything about what it is like to be in a city street?

An argument

The Super Realist painters were more concerned with the paintings themselves than with the scenes they painted. Their work is part of an argument about art. Does a thing have to be beautiful to be art? Can it be beautiful if it is beautifully painted but is about something that is not beautiful? What do you think about this painting? Is it beautiful?

The Allan Stone Gallery, New York

43

Sydney Harbour
Oil crayon and gouache on paper 50 × 38 cm
Ken Done

BORN:
1940

NATIONALITY:
Australian

TYPE OF WORK:
oil paintings, drawings, prints

Photograph Mark Lang/Wildlight Photo Agency

Ken Done is very popular in Australia. On a visit to Sydney you will probably see more of his work than of any other artist. Mostly you will see people wearing his work, for as well as making prints to hang on walls, Ken Done designs tee-shirts, tea-towels, beach bags, calendars, posters, postcards and many other everyday objects.

A mirror to a way of life
Done's work is brightly coloured, busy and fun. It reflects the Australian love of the open air life and the sunshine and blue skies of an Australian summer. Much of his work is about the beach and boats, and looks like a scene at holiday time.

In this busy picture we can see the massive construction of Sydney Harbour bridge which dominates everything. The Opera House with its white sail-like buildings stands out clearly. Ferries travel to and fro across the bay. Yachts of all sizes dot the water. A liner and a cargo ship are moored by the bridge. We see an exciting modern city whose heart is its harbour.

A simple style
Ken Done's style in his drawings (this one was for a calendar) is deceptively simple. For *Sydney Harbour*, Done has used gouache, a thick, opaque paint. He also uses all sorts of clever effects of colour and scale to achieve his effect. Look at the change of scale between the yachts in the foreground and the cargo ship below the bridge. The colours he has chosen are exciting and hot. The bridge and opera house are not really bright pink, but the pink is a very warm colour. The cool blues and greens of the water, splashed with the warmer reflections, emphasise the heat of the air. The white paper showing through is like reflected dazzling light. In contrast the sky is solid blue. A few toy-like clouds will not spoil this perfect summer's day.

Ken Done © 1986

The Making of a Fresco, showing the Building of a City

fresco 5.68 × 9.91 cm

Diego Rivera

LIVED:
1886-1957

NATIONALITY:
Mexican

TYPE OF WORK:
murals, paintings, mosaics

Diego Rivera was a very talented child. At ten years of age he was taking lessons at the art school in Mexico City. At twenty-one he won a scholarship and went to Europe to work. He returned once to Mexico and exhibited his work successfully, but chose to spend the next few years in Europe, working mainly in Paris.

An interest in wall paintings

In 1919, Rivera visited Italy with another Mexican painter, David Siqueiros. They studied Italian paintings and in particular the murals of the fifteenth and sixteenth centuries. In 1921 they decided to return to Mexico City, where Rivera was commissioned to paint a mural at the National Preparatory School. He mastered the technique of fresco painting, putting colour on to wet plaster, and developed a style which was a mixture of the Aztec traditions of the South American Indian people and ideas brought back from Europe.

His reputation spreads

By 1931 Diego Rivera had become well known in the United States. He went to California to paint a mural at the School of Fine Arts, where he chose to work on a large but rather awkwardly shaped space on a stairway. He remembered the Italian three-part murals with triangular tops and he divided his wall into three sections. The painting is a complicated design and contains two views, one seen through the other. The theme is the design and building of a city. In the centre is the giant figure of a worker directing progress. To left and right of him we see the city under construction. In the bottom section the planners and the architects are at work. Over them all is a painting of a scaffold and on it are the fresco painters. Even the supports on the lower section of the wall are part of the painting.

Each of the figures in the picture is a real person. The central figure with the large bottom is Rivera himself. The man in the bowler hat is William Gerstle who commissioned Rivera to make the painting. Rivera's idea of including real people in the work was also learned from his visit to Italy. In the past, painters often included their patrons in their pictures.

The San Francisco Art Institute, California

Some ideas

For city lovers

You may have read this book because you like cities. If so, perhaps you might try drawing the city or town or village in which you live. If you do, you will get to know them better. Remember how Canaletto and Patrick Procktor made so many pictures of Venice? Looking at your hometown and the people who live there with a painter's eyes could help you find out much more about both town and people.

For picture lovers

You may have read this book because you like looking at pictures. If so perhaps you would like to see the original works. Remember that Rauschenberg's interest in painting started with a visit to an art gallery. A list at the front of the book tells you where to find those paintings which are on view to the public. They are in galleries all over the world so you will not be able to see them all. However, your nearest gallery may have other works by the artists you like.

For those who want to have a go themselves

You may have read this book because you like to draw or paint. If so perhaps the book has helped you to discover some of the secrets of picture-making. All the work that is in the book is the result of hard thinking, lots of practice and above all very careful looking. Remember how Madox Brown noticed the workmen, and how Monet visited the railway station? Perhaps you could start a journal now, making a note of places and people and the work that goes on around you. You could collect the information that will help you to make your ideas come alive.

violin

fingerboard geo

volume 1

an intonation, note-reading, theory, shifting system

by barbara barber

© 2008, 2014
Preludio Music Inc.
Estes Park, Colorado

ISBN 0-7390-5026-5

Preludio Music Inc.
exclusively distributed by
Alfred Publishing Co., Inc.
PO Box 10003
Van Nuys, CA 91410-0003

Contents

Introducing Fingerboard Geography in the *Suzuki® Violin School*

The sections and exercises in this book are not intended to be studied from beginning to end. Rather, the teacher should anticipate new Finger Patterns in the student's repertoire, introducing the exercises as needed to prepare the student for new skills and ensure good intonation. Some exercises, such as those involving B♭, E♭ and F♮, would be delayed until needed in the *Suzuki® Violin School, Volume 2*. Below are suggestions for where to introduce the Finger Patterns and exercises found in Parts 1-4 of *Fingerboard Geography*.

While learning *Suzuki® Violin School*	Part 1 12 Finger Patterns	Part 2 Finger Marches	Part 3 Fingerboard Geography	Part 4 No Fear Shifting
Volume 1				
Twinkle - May Song	p. 7, #1 Red	p. 15, #1-4		
Long, Long Ago - Perpetual Motion	p. 7, #2 Blue	p. 15, #5-6 p. 16, #1-4		
Allegretto - Etude	p. 8, #3a Yellow	p. 16, #5-8		
Minuet No. 1 - Gossec Gavotte	p. 8, #4a Green	p. 17, #9-12		
Volume 2				
Chorus - Long, Long Ago	p. 9 #3b Yellow #4b Green	p. 15, #7-8		
Waltz - The Two Grenadiers	p. 9, #5 Orange	p. 17-18, #13-20 p. 19, #1-2	p. 23	
Witches' Dance	p. 12-13 #9 Purple #10 Gold #11 Coral #12 Turquoise	p. 18, #21-24 p. 19, #3-4	p. 24	
Thomas Gavotte - Boccherini Minuet			p. 25	p. 28
Volume 3				
Martini Gavotte - Bach Gavotte in Gm	p. 10-11 #6 Brown #7 Grey #8 Black	p. 19, #5-6 p. 21, #17-18	p. 26	
Humoresque - Becker Gavotte	Review all		Review all	
Bach Gavotte in DM - Bach Bourrée		p. 19-20, #7-12		p. 29 A string
Volume 4				
3 Seitz movements	Review all	p. 20-21, #13-18	Review all	p. 29 D string
2 Vivaldi movements		p. 21, #19-24		p. 30 G string
Bach Double		Review all		p. 30 E string

Principles of Fingerboard Geography

1. Finger Patterns, or intervallic relationships, consist of various vertical combinations of whole-steps and half-steps on the fingerboard.

2. When two or more fingers are placed on the fingerboard, a Finger Pattern must be established.

3. If fewer than four fingers are used, the missing finger/s may be filled in to determine the Finger Pattern.

4. **In all exercises in Parts 1 through 4 of this book, use block fingering, anchoring all fingers wherever possible.** This allows the player to *hear, see,* and *feel* the Finger Patterns.

5. The color assigned to each Finger Pattern reflects the tonality of the pattern.

6. Every string crossing between 2 fingers creates a double-stop. Fingers usually walk, not hop, from one string to another.

7. A Finger Pattern may be played on any one string or combination of two, three, or four strings, producing double-stops and chords.

8. Every double-stop and chord is a Finger Pattern. Remember to fill in any missing fingers to establish questionable patterns.

9. When playing double-stops and chords, the differential, or horizontal distance between the fingers, feels slightly larger, especially in half-steps.

10. A Finger Pattern may be played in any position on the fingerboard.

11. Finger Patterns become proportionately smaller as they move up the fingerboard and larger as they move down. In shifting, the hand frame constantly expands and contracts. Remember to fill in any missing fingers to establish questionable patterns.

12. Finger Patterns are the same on any size violin; only the proportions change.

13. For easy reference, the Finger Pattern charts may be posted in the teacher's studio, the classroom or the student's practice area. We recommend laminating or inserting the charts into plastic sheet protectors for long-term use.

14. Playing the violin in tune is never easy. Hearing, seeing and feeling Finger Patterns can take the guesswork out of intonation and eliminate the need for fingerboard tapes.

15. Finger Patterns are used for life!

Violin Fingerboard Geography, Volume 2 (soon to be published) consists of a review of Finger Patterns and Fingerboard Geography from Volume 1, No Fear Shifting with all four fingers, Double-Stops Made Easy using Finger Patterns, Advanced Finger Pattern Studies in higher positions and Previews for the *Suzuki*® *Violin School,* Volumes 5-10.

Viola Fingerboard Geography, Volumes 1 and 2 (soon to be published) correspond with Violin, Volumes 1 and 2.

String Class Fingerboard Geography (now available) introduces Finger Marches, Four Basic Finger Patterns, Fingerboard Geography and No Fear Shifting for violin, viola, cello and bass, in one simple book.

by Barbara Barber
Published by Preludio Music Inc.
Distributed by Alfred Publishing Co., Inc.

Part 1: Twelve Finger Patterns

The sections and exercises in this book are not intended to be studied from beginning to end. Rather, the teacher should anticipate new Finger Patterns in the student's repertoire, introducing the exercises as needed to prepare the student for new skills and ensure good intonation. See page 4.

To develop quick, precise action in the left hand, these short, "mini-scale" exercises in Part 1 should be played in the middle of the bow – the 8th notes with clean, staccato strokes and the 16th notes with detaché. The tempo is ♩ = 60. We suggest learning each new pattern on the A string, followed by E, D and G strings. Introduction of the Green Pattern, usually the most difficult can be delayed until the students have mastered Red, Blue and Yellow. Follow with the other 8 patterns as needed in the repertoire.

Important: When playing Finger Pattern Exercises, violinists should *always* use block fingering, leaving all fingers anchored. While block fingering is not always used when playing repertoire, keeping fingers anchored in this intonation system allows the student to *see, hear* and *feel* the patterns.

There are many variations that may be used with these Finger Pattern Exercises. Each exercise can be repeated as many times as needed. Students especially enjoy playing them in canon. The 2nd group starts at measure 2:

Repeat as needed

When students become familiar with two or more patterns, they can change the pattern at the top of the ascending scale, then play a different pattern in the descending scale. Go up the scale in Red, stop, lift 2nd finger C♯, move it to C♮, come down the scale in Blue:

Play this first with a stop, then without.

As an introduction to string crossings, double-stops and chords, distribute the fingers on two, three, and four strings.

Blue pattern on two strings:

Blue pattern on three strings:

Blue pattern on four strings:

Keep all fingers anchored!

Keep all fingers anchored!

Keep all fingers anchored!

By changing the Finger Patterns in the ascending/descending scales and distributing the fingers on 1, 2, 3, and 4 strings, a variety of combinations are possible. Be creative!

Four Basic Patterns

1. Red, Twinkle - May Song

2. Blue, Long, Long Ago - Perpetual Motion

3a. Yellow with "Hot Pink" 3, Allegretto - Etude
The 3rd finger in this pattern sounds, looks and feels very different!

Anchor all fingers

4a. Green, Minuet No. 1 - Gossec Gavotte

Anchor all fingers

3b. Yellow with "Hot Pink" 3, Chorus - Long, Long Ago (Vol. 2)
This pattern is often played in 1st Position beginning on low 1st finger.

Anchor all fingers

4b. Green
This pattern is often played in 1st Position beginning on low 1st finger.

Anchor all fingers

Contractions

5. Orange, Waltz - The Two Grenadiers

Anchor all fingers

6. Brown, Martini Gavotte - Bach Gavotte in G Minor

Augmented 2nds

9. Purple, Witches' Dance

Anchor all fingers

10. Gold

Anchor all fingers

Augmented 2nd Extensions

11. Coral

12. Turquoise

Part 2: Finger Marches

The sections and exercises in this book are not intended to be studied from beginning to end. Rather, the teacher should anticipate new Finger Patterns in the student's repertoire, introducing the exercises as needed to prepare the him or her for new skills and ensure good intonation. See page 4.

In this section, fingers should be placed independently. Remember that accidentals carry through the measure and repeated patterns will use the same fingerings.

The 1st finger is the "home base" note on which all Finger Patterns are built. The 1st Finger Marches in this section establish the violinist's left hand placement in 1st position with the "high" 1st finger and teach the hand to move across the fingerboard from high strings to low and back again. 1st Finger Marches are excellent for beginning string students or those who have just moved to a larger size instrument.

Finger Marches may be played between any open string and 2nd, 3rd or 4th fingers, between any 2 fingers, and in any position. They can also be played on 1, 2 or 3 strings only. Later, 1st Finger Marches using the "low" 1st finger may be introduced. Mixed 1st Marches alternate between the high and low 1st fingers, zigzagging diagonally across the strings. Zigzagging Finger Marches are especially useful when students encounter *changing* Finger Patterns such those below in which a finger moves diagonally across the fingerboard. Two, four and eight note slurs may be added; the 8th notes may be doubled to 16th notes. Teachers and students can invent Finger Marches as needed in the repertoire. Here are a few examples:

Symbols

x4	Extended 4th finger
*	Place finger independently
1————	Keep finger anchored
1————↑	Release anchored finger as new finger is placed

Finger Marches

Rotate the left arm to the right to reach the G string, then back to the left to return to the E

5. Long, Long Ago - Perpetual Motion

7. Chorus - Long, Long Ago (Vol. 2)

Play No. 4 again before No. 8

16

The Major/Minor Difference

1. Long, Long Ago - Perpetual Motion

5. Allegretto - Etude

9. Minuet No. 1 - Gossec Gavotte

10.

11.

12.

13. Waltz - The Two Grenadiers

14.

15.

16.

18

21. Witches' Dance

Mixed Finger Marches

In these exercises, one finger moves diagonally across the strings.

A & E Strings, Waltz - The Two Grenadiers

1.

2.

D & A Strings, Witches' Dance

3.

4.

G & D Strings, Martini Gavotte - Bach Gavotte in G Minor

5.

6.

7. Dominant 7th Arpeggios on A & E, Bach Gavotte in D - Bach Bourrée

8.

20

13. Dominant 7th Arpeggios on D & A, Seitz movements

19. Dominant 7th Arpeggios on G & D, Vivaldi movements

Part 3: Fingerboard Geography

The sections and exercises in this book are not intended to be studied from beginning to end. Rather, the teacher should anticipate new Finger Patterns in the student's repertoire, introducing the exercises as needed to prepare the student for new skills and ensure good intonation. See page 4.

This section introduces all of the notes in 1st position for violin. The tempo is ♩ = 60 and the exercises should be played with full, legato bow strokes. Students should "see and say" the note names before playing each pair of notes in the left column. Next the students "see and say" the distance on the fingerboard in the center column, then play. Finally the students "see and say" the name of the interval in the right column, then play. These three steps can be introduced over a period of days, weeks, or months, depending on the level of the students and the frequency of lessons/classes. When the students have learned the information in all three columns, go to the same exercises on page 26, naming notes, distances and intervals by reading the notes only. For variety, go around a circle or down a row of students, asking each to name either note names, distance on the fingerboard or name of the interval, then everyone plays the pair of notes. Later, the first student says the note names, the second student says the distance on the fingerboard, the third student says the name of the interval, then all play the pair of notes. In a class of mixed levels, less advanced students can say note names and more advanced ones say distance and interval.

When playing Fingerboard Geography, care must be taken to ensure smooth and efficient finger actions such as anchoring and sliding chromatically. Keep the 1st finger anchored on the lower string for the first line as shown below, and on both strings for the second line. The Major 3rd and tri-tone intervals in the first line can be filled in with the missing fingers as shown, to establish these patterns. The 2nd and 3rd fingers will stay anchored as they are placed in the second line. The 2nd and 3rd fingers should slide on the upper string in chromatic motions such as G to G♯, then remain anchored. When playing G♯ to A, the 2nd finger should "touch and lift" – the 3rd is placed, then 2nd is lifted; likewise with A♯ to B.

A & E Strings, Waltz - The Two Grenadiers

Note Names & Location on the Staff	Distance on the Fingerboard	Name of the Interval
B C	½ step	minor 2nd
B C#	whole-step	Major 2nd
B D	1½ steps	minor 3rd
B D#	2 whole-steps	Major 3rd
B E	2½ steps	Perfect 4th
B E#	3 whole-steps	Tri-tone (Augmented 4th to E#, Diminished 5th to F♮)
B F#	straight across	Perfect 5th
B G	½ step	minor 6th
B G#	whole-step	Major 6th
B A	1½ steps	minor 7th
B A#	2 whole-steps	Major 7th
B B	2½ steps	Perfect 8va (octave)

D & A Strings, Witches' Dance

Note Names & Location on the Staff	Distance on the Fingerboard	Name of the Interval
E F	½ step	minor 2nd
E F#	whole-step	Major 2nd
E G	1½ steps	minor 3rd
E G#	2 whole-steps	Major 3rd
E A	2½ steps	Perfect 4th
E A#	3 whole-steps	Tri-tone (Augmented 4th to A#, Diminished 5th to B♭)
E B	straight across	Perfect 5th
E C	½ step	minor 6th
E C#	whole-step	Major 6th
E D	1½ steps	minor 7th
E D#	2 whole-steps	Major 7th
E E	2½ steps	Perfect 8va (octave)

Note Names & Location on the Staff	Distance on the Fingerboard	Name of the Interval
A Bb	½ step	minor 2nd
A B♮	whole-step	Major 2nd
A C	1½ steps	minor 3rd
A C#	2 whole-steps	Major 3rd
A D	2½ steps	Perfect 4th
A D#	3 whole-steps	Tri-tone (Augmented 4th to D#, Diminished 5th to Eb)
A E	straight across	Perfect 5th
A F	½ step	minor 6th
A F#	whole-step	Major 6th
A G	1½ steps	minor 7th
A G#	2 whole-steps	Major 7th
A A	2½ steps	Perfect 8va (octave)

Fingerboard Geography on A, D & G Strings
Martini Gavotte - Bach Gavottes in D Major

♩ = 60

A and E Strings starting on B

D and A Strings starting on E

G and D Strings starting on A

Part 4: No Fear Shifting
with Fingerboard Geography

The sections and exercises in this book are not intended to be studied from beginning to end. Rather, the teacher should anticipate new shifts in the student's repertoire, introducing the exercises as needed to prepare the student for new skills and ensure good intonation. See page 4.

When introducing shifting, the violinist's left hand should be loose and relaxed, gliding easily up and down the fingerboard. Harmonic Exercises one page 28 relieve any left hand tension and should be played with full, legato bows. They can be played with all four Basic Finger Patterns. Next, repeat Fingerboard Geography, an already familiar exercise, with shifts on pages 29 and 30. The first time this shifting system is used, the student will shift all the way to 8th position! The violinist's left arm should rotate to the right, bringing the hand up and on top of the instrument for the high positions. In group lessons, less advanced students can play the exercises in one position, providing a solid tonal foundation, while more advanced ones learn to shift. These exercises can be started on any finger and transposed into any position. Once learned, they are easily played by rote. Some examples:

Shifting 2nd to 9th Position:

Etc.

Shifting 3rd to 10th Position:

Etc.

Combining Finger Patterns with Fingerboard Geography
With imagination, teachers and students can combine shifts and patterns in dozens of different ways.

Shift a minor 3rd, then play the Red Finger Pattern:

Shift a Perfect 5th, then play the Yellow Finger Pattern:

Shifting to Harmonics, Thomas Gavotte - Boccherini Minuet
Play with all 4 Basic Finger Patterns

♩ = 60

A String

D String

G String

E String

No Fear Shifting With 1st Finger

30

G String, 2 Vivaldi movements

E String, Bach Double

Part 5: Fingerboard Geography for the
Suzuki® Violin School, Volumes 1- 4

This part consists of practice spots and preview suggestions for most of the pieces in the *Suzuki® Violin School, Volumes 1-4*. The Revised Editions from 2008 onward have been used. The following suggestions will aid the student, parent and teacher in learning these exercises:

- Use these exercises in conjunction with the Finger Exercises found in the *Suzuki® Violin School*.
- Start the previews well before the student begins playing each piece. Play each preview slowly and carefully and repeat it many times.
- Check key signatures carefully.
- Finger Patterns colors are noted when used for the first time. Be sure to learn these from Part I before encountering them in the previews. Colors are also indicated in certain instances, especially when the Finger Patterns are changing.
- Refer to the explanation of the symbols below and observe them carefully.
- *Play* all guide notes. See below for an explanation of ♩ and (♩).
- Where fingerings have been changed, the author's fingerings are on the top and printed fingerings on the bottom.

While *Violin Fingerboard Geography, Volume 1* is a left hand technique book, some preview suggestions for right arm skills are also included. Teachers have their own favorite preview exercises, however, and blank staves are available for teachers to add their own.

Symbols

✳	Place finger independently
×4	Extended 4th finger
1————	Keep finger anchored
1————↑	Release anchored finger as new finger is placed
1 / 3 ===↑	Release anchored fingers as new finger is placed
⌐ or [	Cover a 5th with the finger
∧ or ∨	½ Step
W or M	Whole Step
⌐∧⌐ or ⌐∨⌐	1½ Steps or Augmented 2nd
♩ ♩ (1 – 1)	Slide or shift the finger
♩̸ = ♫♫	
1 2 3 (●) or (● ● ●)	Set guide note or notes for practice
1 2 3 ● or ● ● ●	Set guide note or notes for life!
♩ ♩ (1 2)	Repeat notes 3-4 times, anchoring fingers

Suzuki® Violin School, Volume 1

1 Twinkle Variation A, m. 5

A Major Scale

2 Folk Song - Lightly Row

m. 1

m. 7

3 Folk Song - Song of the Wind

m. 3

5 Folk Song - O Come, Little Children

Up   bow   goes   my   bow   'til   it   comes   to   a   stop!

m. 1

m. 9

Set 3 independently

m. 13

m. 9

7 **Bayly - Long, Long Ago**

m. 9

Hop

Hop

Variations for G Major Scale

A. B. C. D.

34

36

Suzuki® Violin School, Volume 2

1 Handel - Chorus from "Judas Maccabaeus"
m. 12-13

Yellow
Anchor all fingers

m. 11

Set 3, retake bow

2 Bach - Musette
m. 9

Anchor all fingers

Anchor all fingers

M3rd

m. 8

M3rd

3 Weber - Hunters' Chorus
m. 1 & 5

m. 4

m. 15

m. 19

m. 25

4 Bayly - Long, Long Ago
m. 1

Practice with G/D drone, anchoring fingers on A string

Etc.

Variation, m. 17

Anchor fingers on A string

Etc.

8 Paganini - Theme from *Witches' Dance*

m. 1

9 Thomas - Gavotte from *Mignon*

m. 7

41

B♭ Major Scale & Arpeggio

44

12 Boccherini - Minuet

Suzuki® Violin School, Volume 3

3 Bach - Gavotte in G Minor

4 Dvorak - Humoresque

50

m. 9-16

Bourrée II, m. 1

52

Suzuki® Violin School, Volume 4

1 Seitz - Concerto No. 2, 3rd Movt.   m. 10

m. 84-95

m. 107

2 Seitz - Concerto No. 5, 1st movt.

m. 23

m. 25

Move 1st diagonally

Gold

m. 23

m. 43

m. 45

m. 43

Green

m. 49

E Major Scale & Arpeggio

Yellow   Yellow

m. 52-59

Play without slurs, then with

m. 80

m. 90   m. 90

Without, then with slurs

m. 94

3 Seitz - Concerto No. 5, 3rd Movt.   m. 15

Twinkle Variation A, lower half, spiccato   Etc.   m3rd   M3rd   m3rd   M3rd

m. 13-26

Lower half, spiccato

m. 84

56

Preparation for Double Stops

Anchor all finger*s*

m. 117-141 in Half Notes

m. 117-141 as written

Without, then with slurs

m. 146

Purple

m. 165

58

4 Vivaldi/Nachéz - Concerto in A Minor, 1st Movt.

60

5 Vivaldi/Nachéz - Concerto in A Minor, 3rd Movt.

62

With more than 40 years of performing and teaching experience, violinist and violist Barbara Barber joined the sales team at Robertson & Sons Violin Shop, one of the world's premier bowed string instrument dealers, in Albuquerque, NM in 2014. She has concertized and presented master classes and pedagogy clinics across the United States, and in Canada, Mexico, El Salvador, Brazil, Peru, Colombia, Australia, New Zealand, Korea, Taiwan, Hong Kong, Japan, Italy, Ireland, Finland, Sweden and Bermuda. She received her Bachelor of Music and Master of Music in performance at Texas Tech University with additional studies at Interlochen Music Camp, Rocky Ridge Music Center, Accademia di Chigiana in Italy, Taos School of Music and Banff Centre. Barbara has held faculty appointments at Texas Tech University, Texas Christian University and the University of Colorado. She has been recognized for her many articles, presentations and roles on the advisory and editorial boards of the American Strings Teachers Association and the Suzuki Association of the Americas. Barbara's widely-used collections of books and CDs are published by Preludio Music Inc. and distributed worldwide by Alfred Music.